# PRAYER FORMED BY THE WORD OF GOD

Scripture-Based Prayers for Wisdom, Peace, Strength, Healing, Purpose, Families, Leadership, and Spiritual Growth

**Steven Robertson Sr.**

Steps On Purpose

Prayer Formed by the Word of God



Scripture quotations are taken from the New King James Version® (NKJV) and the Holy Bible, New Living Translation® (NLT), unless otherwise indicated.

Published by Steps On Purpose Publishing

Milwaukee, Wisconsin

Print ISBN: 978-1-972165-00-3

E-book ISBN: 978-1-972165-01-0

Printed in the United States of America.

# DEDICATION

Dedicated to every believer seeking to grow deeper in prayer, wisdom, peace, spiritual maturity, and relationship with God.

May the Word of God strengthen your faith, renew your mind, guide your steps, and shape your prayer life for generations to come.

# TABLE OF CONTENTS

# INTRODUCTION

Prayer is more than a religious activity. Prayer is relationship with God.

Through prayer, believers seek wisdom, receive peace, surrender burdens, grow spiritually, renew the mind, gain direction, and align the heart with the will of God.

Yet many believers struggle with prayer. Some feel uncertain about what to say. Some feel inconsistent. Some pray mostly from pressure, fear, or emotion. Others want to pray Scripture but do not know where to begin.

This book was written to help believers develop a prayer life formed by the Word of God.

When prayer is shaped by Scripture, believers learn to pray from truth instead of fear, from faith instead of panic, and from relationship instead of striving.

The prayers throughout the New Testament epistles reveal a strong pattern of spiritually mature prayer. They focus on wisdom, revelation, love, discernment, strength, endurance, unity, and spiritual growth.

These prayers teach believers to pray beyond temporary circumstances and grow from the inside out.

This guide includes teaching, prayers, declarations, reflection prompts, corporate prayers, epistle prayer forms, blessings, and daily prayer rhythms. It is designed for personal devotion, group prayer, mentoring, family prayer, leadership settings, and spiritual growth.

The goal is not perfection.

The goal is growth.

As you move through these pages, take your time. Pray slowly. Reflect honestly. Let the Word of God renew your mind, strengthen your faith, and shape your prayer life one step at a time.

# HOW TO USE THIS BOOK

This book is designed to help you pray Scripture with clarity, confidence, and consistency.

You may use it for personal devotion, Bible study, prayer groups, mentoring, leadership gatherings, family devotion, or corporate prayer.

You do not need to rush. Some chapters may be prayed through in one sitting. Others may be revisited over several days or during specific seasons of life.

Each chapter includes:

## Foundation Scriptures

- A brief teaching
- A Scripture-based prayer

## Declarations

- Reflection questions
- A corporate prayer
- A closing encouragement
- The prayers may be prayed exactly as written or adapted personally. For example, "Father, strengthen Your people" may become "Father, strengthen me," "strengthen my family," or "strengthen our church."
- The appendices provide additional tools, including epistle prayers, declarations, corporate prayer models, and daily prayer rhythms.
- Approach this book with openness, humility, and expectation. Let Scripture shape your thinking. Let

prayer strengthen your faith. Let the Holy Spirit guide you as you grow in relationship with God.

- You may use it for personal devotion, Bible study, prayer groups, mentoring, leadership gatherings, family devotion, or corporate prayer.
- You do not need to rush. Some chapters may be prayed through in one sitting. Others may be revisited over several days or during specific seasons of life.
- Each chapter includes:

## Foundation Scriptures

- A brief teaching
- A Scripture-based prayer

## Declarations

- Reflection questions
- A corporate prayer
- A closing encouragement
- The prayers may be prayed exactly as written or adapted personally. For example, "Father, strengthen Your people" may become "Father, strengthen me," "strengthen my family," or "strengthen our church."
- The appendices provide additional tools, including epistle prayers, declarations, corporate prayer models, and daily prayer rhythms.
- Approach this book with openness, humility, and expectation. Let Scripture shape your thinking. Let

prayer strengthen your faith. Let the Holy Spirit guide you as you grow in relationship with God.

- Section I
- Foundations of Scripture-Formed Prayer

# SECTION I

# FOUNDATIONS OF SCRIPTURE-FORMED PRAYER

Prayer becomes stronger when it is rooted in truth.

Before believers pray about life, decisions, healing, leadership, peace, and purpose, they must understand what God has already provided through His Word.

These prayers are designed to help believers pray from faith instead of fear and from spiritual confidence instead of uncertainty.

# CHAPTER 1

# DECLARING THE BLESSING OF THE LORD

## Foundation Scriptures

- Ephesians 1:3
- Galatians 3:13–14

## Numbers 6:24–26

Deuteronomy 28:1–14

Psalm 23

Proverbs 10:22

## Opening Encouragement

The blessing of God is more than provision. It includes grace, peace, wisdom, protection, purpose, favor, redemption, and the presence of God working in and through our lives.

Prayer helps believers agree with what God has spoken and walk with confidence in what Christ has made available.

## Teaching

Ephesians 1:3 says that God has blessed us with every spiritual blessing in heavenly places in Christ. Through

Jesus Christ, believers have been redeemed, accepted, forgiven, and brought into relationship with God.

The blessing of the Lord touches every area of life. It shapes how we think, how we serve, how we lead, how we give, and how we trust God during pressure.

This blessing is not about selfish ambition. It is about living under the wisdom, grace, and favor of God so that our lives can glorify Him and bless others.

## Prayer

Father,

Thank You that through Jesus Christ I have been redeemed and brought into the blessing You have provided.

Thank You that I am blessed with every spiritual blessing in heavenly places in Christ.

Lead me with wisdom.

Guide me with peace.

Strengthen me with grace.

Order my steps according to Your Word.

I declare that I am blessed in my going out and blessed in my coming in.

I am blessed in my home, my work, my relationships, and the purpose You have entrusted to me.

Strengthen the work of my hands.

Teach me to walk in humility, generosity, integrity, discipline, and faithfulness.

Thank You that You supply all my needs according to Your riches in glory by Christ Jesus.

Thank You that Your favor surrounds me like a shield.

Let my household be marked by wisdom, love, protection, unity, and spiritual strength.

Use my life to bring hope, healing, encouragement, and truth to others.

Be glorified in every part of my life.

In Jesus' name,

Amen.

## Declarations

- I am blessed in Christ Jesus.
- God's wisdom directs my life.
- My steps are ordered by the Lord.
- God strengthens the work of my hands.
- My household is blessed and protected.
- I walk in wisdom, clarity, and purpose.
- The favor of the Lord surrounds me.
- The blessing of the Lord flows through my life to others.

## Reflect and Respond

- Where do you need to renew your thinking about God's blessing?

- Are you praying from fear or from confidence in Christ?
- How can your life become a greater blessing to others?
- What promise from God's Word will you begin declaring consistently?

## Corporate Prayer

Father,

We thank You that You have blessed Your people in Christ.

Let Your wisdom, peace, favor, and grace rest upon our lives, families, homes, churches, and communities.

Strengthen the work You have called us to do.

Teach us to walk in humility, generosity, wisdom, and faithfulness.

May the Lord bless us and keep us.

May the Lord make His face shine upon us and give us peace.

In Jesus' name,

Amen.

# CHAPTER 2

# PRAYER FOR WISDOM AND CLARITY

## Foundation Scriptures

- James 1:5
- Ephesians 1:17–18
- Proverbs 3:5–6
- Colossians 1:9
- Psalm 32:8
- Isaiah 30:21

## Opening Encouragement

There are seasons in life when people need more than motivation. They need wisdom.

Decisions, responsibilities, relationships, leadership, opportunities, and unexpected pressures can leave the mind overwhelmed and uncertain. Yet Scripture reminds believers that God is willing to guide those who seek Him with humility and trust.

## Teaching

James 1 teaches that if anyone lacks wisdom, they can ask God, who gives generously.

God does not shame His people for needing wisdom. He invites them to ask.

Wisdom protects decisions, relationships, emotions, priorities, leadership, and spiritual growth.

Prayer rooted in the Word helps believers slow down, become spiritually sensitive, and trust God's leadership one step at a time.

## Prayer

Father,

Thank You that You are a God of wisdom, understanding, clarity, and direction.

Your Word says that if anyone lacks wisdom, they may ask You, and You give generously.

So Father, I ask You for wisdom today.

Give me wisdom for every responsibility, relationship, decision, opportunity, and challenge before me.

Open the eyes of my understanding.

Help me see clearly and respond wisely.

Remove confusion, fear, distraction, and unnecessary pressure from my thinking.

Quiet anxious thoughts.

Help me hear Your direction clearly.

Strengthen my discernment.

Guard me from impulsive decisions and unnecessary distractions.

Surround me with wise counsel and spiritually healthy voices.

Renew my mind through the Word of God.

Thank You that the Holy Spirit leads and guides me.

Teach me to walk by faith, wisdom, humility, and obedience.

In Jesus' name,

Amen.

## Declarations

- God gives me wisdom generously.
- My steps are ordered by the Lord.
- The Holy Spirit leads and guides me.
- I walk in wisdom, clarity, and discernment.
- God is not the author of confusion.
- The peace of God guards my heart and mind.
- I trust the Lord with all my heart.
- Wisdom and understanding grow within me daily.

## Reflect and Respond

- What areas of your life currently require wisdom and clarity?
- What distractions may be interfering with discernment?
- How can you become more intentional about seeking God daily?
- What next step of obedience may God already be showing you?

## Corporate Prayer

Father,

We thank You for being a God of wisdom, peace, and understanding.

Guide Your people throughout every area of life.

Remove confusion, fear, distraction, and instability.

Teach us to trust You and acknowledge You in all our ways.

Let wisdom govern our decisions, relationships, and priorities.

In Jesus' name,

Amen.

# CHAPTER 3

# PRAYER FOR PURPOSE AND DIRECTION

## Foundation Scriptures

- Jeremiah 29:11
- Proverbs 3:5–6
- Psalm 37:23
- Romans 8:14
- Ephesians 2:10

## Opening Encouragement

Many people desire clarity concerning purpose, direction, timing, and next steps.

Purpose is not discovered through panic, comparison, or striving. It grows through relationship with God, spiritual maturity, wisdom, and obedience.

## Teaching

God directs the steps of those who trust Him.

The Holy Spirit helps believers recognize wisdom, peace, discernment, and healthy direction. Purpose is not only about achievement. It is about becoming people who reflect the character of Christ.

Prayer helps believers stop living reactively and begin walking intentionally.

## Prayer

Father,

Thank You that You are faithful to lead and guide my life.

Order my steps according to Your wisdom and purpose.

Help me trust You with every season, opportunity, transition, and unanswered question.

Remove confusion, fear, insecurity, comparison, and unnecessary striving.

Teach me to walk faithfully in what You have already placed before me.

Lead me by Your Spirit.

Open the right doors according to Your purpose.

Close doors that are not aligned with Your will.

Surround me with wise counsel and healthy relationships.

Renew my mind through the Word of God.

Help me use my gifts, opportunities, leadership, and influence wisely.

Let my life reflect the character of Jesus Christ.

In Jesus' name,

Amen.

## Declarations

- God directs my steps faithfully.

- The Holy Spirit leads and guides me.
- My life has purpose in Christ.
- God opens the right doors at the right time.
- I trust the Lord with my future.
- My mind is renewed through the Word of God.
- I walk intentionally and faithfully.
- God gives clarity concerning purpose and direction.

## Reflect and Respond

- What areas of your life currently require direction?
- Are you trying to force answers that require patience?
- What distractions or comparisons need to be surrendered?
- What next step of obedience may God already be showing you?

## Corporate Prayer

Father,

Guide Your people throughout every season of life.

Strengthen leaders, families, students, mentors, and believers with clarity, peace, wisdom, and discernment.

Remove confusion, fear, and unhealthy striving.

Help Your people walk faithfully in every assignment You have entrusted to them.

In Jesus' name,

Amen.

# CHAPTER 4

# PRAYER FOR SPIRITUAL STRENGTH DURING PRESSURE

## Foundation Scriptures

- 1 Corinthians 10:13
- 2 Corinthians 12:9
- Ephesians 6:10–18
- James 1:12
- Philippians 1:6

## Opening Encouragement

Every believer experiences seasons of pressure, weakness, temptation, discouragement, or uncertainty.

Yet Scripture continually reminds believers that God provides grace, wisdom, endurance, and strength.

## Teaching

God's grace is sufficient during every season.

Spiritual strength grows through dependence upon God, not self-sufficiency.

Prayer helps believers remain spiritually grounded instead of emotionally overwhelmed.

## Prayer

Father,

Thank You that Your grace is sufficient for me.

Strengthen me inwardly through the Holy Spirit.

Help me remain spiritually grounded during seasons of pressure, temptation, weakness, and discouragement.

Thank You that You are faithful and always provide wisdom and a way of escape.

Renew my mind through the Word of God.

Guard my heart and mind with peace.

Help me remain strong in the Lord and in the power of Your might.

When I feel weak, remind me that Your grace sustains me.

When I feel discouraged, strengthen me with hope.

Teach me to trust You deeply during difficult seasons.

Continue the work You have begun within me.

In Jesus' name,

Amen.

## Declarations

- The grace of God is sufficient for me.
- God strengthens me inwardly.
- I am strong in the Lord.
- God provides wisdom and a way of escape.
- The peace of God guards my heart and mind.
- God will never leave me nor forsake me.
- Fear and discouragement do not control me.

- God sustains me through every season.

## Reflect and Respond

- What pressures are currently affecting your peace?
- Are there areas where you need greater dependence upon God?
- What temptations or distractions require wisdom?
- What would change if you trusted God's grace more deeply?

## Corporate Prayer

Father,

Strengthen Your people throughout every season of pressure, temptation, uncertainty, and spiritual warfare.

Guard hearts and minds with peace.

Help believers walk in wisdom, endurance, humility, and spiritual maturity.

Strengthen us inwardly through the Holy Spirit.

In Jesus' name,

Amen.

# CHAPTER 5

# PRAYER FOR HEALING AND RESTORATION

## Foundation Scriptures

- Isaiah 53:4–5
- Psalm 103:1–5
- Joel 2:25
- Philippians 4:6–7
- Jeremiah 30:17

## Opening Encouragement

God is a God of healing, renewal, mercy, and restoration.

Healing touches more than the body. God also restores hearts, minds, relationships, hope, peace, and spiritual strength.

## Teaching

The work of Jesus Christ touches every part of human brokenness.

Healing and restoration are not always instant, but God remains faithful throughout the process.

Prayer helps believers bring every wounded area honestly before God.

## Prayer

Father,

Thank You that You are a God of healing, restoration, mercy, and peace.

Heal what is broken.

Restore what has become weary.

Renew my heart, mind, emotions, and spirit.

Where there has been anxiety, bring peace.

Where there has been grief, bring comfort.

Where there has been disappointment, bring hope.

Teach me to trust You during the process of healing and restoration.

Help me release bitterness, fear, shame, and hopelessness.

Strengthen every weak area of my life.

Thank You that Your mercy is new every morning.

Thank You that Your grace sustains me daily.

In Jesus' name,

Amen.

## Declarations

- God is my Healer and Restorer.
- The peace of God guards my heart and mind.
- God renews my strength daily.
- I walk in peace, healing, and restoration.

- God restores what has been broken.
- My mind is renewed through the Word of God.
- The Holy Spirit strengthens me inwardly.
- God's grace sustains me daily.

## Reflect and Respond

- What areas of your life currently need healing or restoration?
- What fears or disappointments need to be surrendered?
- How can you cooperate with the healing process spiritually and practically?
- What promises from Scripture strengthen your faith?

## Corporate Prayer

Father,

Bring healing and peace throughout homes, families, churches, and communities.

Strengthen those who are weary, grieving, discouraged, wounded, or anxious.

Restore hope, peace, wisdom, and spiritual strength.

May the peace of God guard hearts and minds throughout every season of healing and restoration.

In Jesus' name,

Amen.

# CHAPTER 6

# PRAYER FOR PEACE, TRUST, AND FREEDOM FROM ANXIETY

## Foundation Scriptures

- Philippians 4:6–8
- Isaiah 26:3
- 1 Peter 5:7
- Matthew 6:25–34
- John 14:27

## Opening Encouragement

Many people carry silent pressure every day.

Concerns about family, finances, health, responsibilities, and the future can weigh heavily upon the heart and mind. Yet God continually invites His people to trust Him.

## Teaching

Peace grows where trust grows.

Prayer helps believers release burdens into God's hands and remain spiritually steady during uncertain seasons.

The Word of God renews the mind and helps believers respond with wisdom instead of panic.

## Prayer

Father,

Thank You that You are faithful, present, wise, and trustworthy.

Today I bring every burden, fear, pressure, uncertainty, and anxious thought before You.

Teach me to trust You more deeply.

Help me release what I cannot control.

Guard my heart and mind with peace.

Quiet anxious thoughts.

Renew my thinking through the Word of God.

Help me walk in wisdom instead of fear.

Where there has been confusion, bring clarity.

Where there has been emotional exhaustion, bring renewal.

Thank You that I do not have the spirit of fear, but of power, love, and a sound mind.

Teach me to trust Your timing and Your faithfulness.

Thank You that Your peace surpasses understanding and guards my heart and mind.

In Jesus' name,

Amen.

## Declarations

- The peace of God guards my heart and mind.

- I refuse to be ruled by fear or anxiety.
- God is my refuge and strength.
- I cast my cares upon the Lord.
- I have the mind of Christ.
- God has not given me the spirit of fear.
- I walk in peace, wisdom, and stability.
- The grace of God sustains me daily.

## Reflect and Respond

- What burdens or fears are currently affecting your peace?
- Are your thoughts being shaped more by fear or by truth?
- What situations currently require deeper trust?
- How can you become more intentional about renewing your mind daily?

## Corporate Prayer

Father,

Guard hearts and minds throughout homes, families, churches, workplaces, and communities.

Strengthen those who are weary, fearful, discouraged, or overwhelmed.

Renew minds through the truth of Your Word.

Teach Your people to trust You deeply during every season of life.

In Jesus' name,

Amen.

# SECTION II

## DAILY PRAYER RHYTHMS

Prayer is not only for moments of crisis.

Prayer is meant to become part of the rhythm of everyday life.

Morning prayer helps believers begin the day with wisdom, surrender, and intentionality. Evening prayer helps believers release burdens and rest in the peace and faithfulness of God.

# CHAPTER 7

# MORNING PRAYER FORMED BY THE WORD

## Foundation Scriptures

- Psalm 63:1–3
- Lamentations 3:22–23
- Romans 12:1–2
- James 1:5
- Psalm 119:105

## Opening Encouragement

How believers begin the day often shapes how they respond throughout the day.

Morning prayer helps believers begin with gratitude, wisdom, surrender, peace, and spiritual focus before pressure and distractions begin competing for attention.

## Teaching

Throughout Scripture, believers consistently sought God early.

Morning prayer is not about religious routine. It is about beginning the day with spiritual awareness and dependence upon God.

Prayer and Scripture help renew the mind, strengthen peace, and align the heart with wisdom and truth.

## Prayer

Father,

Thank You for this new day.

Thank You for Your mercy, grace, wisdom, and faithfulness.

Your mercies are new every morning.

Great is Your faithfulness.

Father, lead me and guide me throughout this day.

Order my steps according to Your wisdom.

Renew my mind through the Word of God.

Help me not to be conformed to this world, but transformed by the renewing of my mind.

Give me wisdom for every responsibility, conversation, opportunity, and decision before me.

Guard my heart and mind with peace.

Strengthen me to walk with humility, discernment, patience, and love.

Help me reflect the character of Jesus Christ throughout this day.

Thank You that Your angels are encamped around about me.

Thank You that You are faithful to guide, strengthen, and sustain me.

In Jesus' name,

Amen.

## Declarations

- God's mercies are new every morning.
- My steps are ordered by the Lord.
- The Holy Spirit leads and guides me.
- I walk in wisdom, peace, and discernment.
- My mind is renewed through the Word of God.
- God strengthens me throughout this day.
- I reflect the character of Jesus Christ.
- The peace of God guards my heart and mind.

## Reflect and Respond

- What mindset do you want to begin this day with?
- What distractions need to be surrendered early?
- How can you become more intentional throughout your day?
- What truth from Scripture do you need to carry with you today?

## Corporate Prayer

Father,

Thank You for new mercies and new grace today.

Guide Your people throughout every responsibility, relationship, assignment, and opportunity.

Strengthen homes, families, leaders, students, pastors, teachers, and communities with wisdom and peace.

Help us walk intentionally and faithfully throughout this day.

In Jesus' name,

Amen.

# CHAPTER 8

# EVENING PRAYER OF THANKSGIVING AND SURRENDER

## Foundation Scriptures

- Philippians 4:6–7
- Psalm 4:8
- 1 John 1:9
- Ephesians 4:31–32
- Psalm 121

## Opening Encouragement

Evening prayer helps believers end the day with peace instead of emotional heaviness.

Rather than carrying anxiety, frustration, regret, or fear into the night, believers are invited to surrender burdens honestly before God.

## Teaching

Scripture teaches believers to cast their cares upon the Lord and trust Him with every concern.

Evening prayer creates space for:

gratitude

reflection

forgiveness

surrender

peace

spiritual renewal

Rest becomes healthier when the heart is surrendered and the mind is anchored in truth.

## Prayer

Father,

Thank You for carrying me throughout this day.

Thank You for Your faithfulness, protection, wisdom, and grace.

Tonight I release every burden, pressure, disappointment, anxious thought, and unfinished concern into Your hands.

Guard my heart and mind with peace.

Help me not carry fear, bitterness, offense, or emotional heaviness into this night.

Teach me to forgive quickly.

If I have failed, missed the mark, or responded poorly today, thank You for Your mercy and grace.

Renew my mind through the Word of God.

Give me peaceful rest and sweet sleep.

Protect my household, my family, and those connected to my life.

Thank You that You neither slumber nor sleep.

Thank You that You are faithful in every season.

In Jesus' name,

Amen.

## Declarations

- The peace of God guards my heart and mind.
- I release every burden into God's hands.
- God gives me peace and rest.
- My household is protected by the Lord.
- I choose forgiveness and peace.
- God is faithful in every season.
- My mind is renewed through the Word of God.
- I rest in the faithfulness of God.

## Reflect and Respond

- What burdens need to be released before rest?
- Are there offenses or frustrations that need forgiveness?
- What moments of grace or gratitude did you experience today?
- How can you become more intentional about ending the day in peace?

## Corporate Prayer

Father,

Thank You for Your faithfulness throughout this day.

Bring peace, rest, protection, and renewal throughout homes, families, churches, and communities.

Strengthen those who are weary, anxious, discouraged, or emotionally overwhelmed.

Guard hearts and minds with peace.

And help Your people rest in Your goodness and faithfulness.

In Jesus' name,

Amen.

## SECTION CLOSING ENCOURAGEMENT

Prayer is not meant to become rushed, mechanical, or disconnected from relationship.

Small moments of daily prayer, surrender, gratitude, and Scripture meditation help believers remain spiritually grounded one day at a time.

Morning by morning.

Day by day.

Step by step.

# SECTION III

# RELATIONSHIPS, FAMILY, AND COMMUNITY

Prayer strengthens more than individuals.

It also strengthens homes, families, relationships, leaders, communities, and future generations.

These prayers are designed to help believers pray for unity, wisdom, healing, peace, and spiritual growth throughout the relationships connected to everyday life.

# CHAPTER 9

# PRAYER FOR FAMILIES AND HOUSEHOLDS

## Foundation Scriptures

- Acts 16:31
- Joshua 24:15
- Proverbs 22:6
- Psalm 127:1–3
- Ephesians 6:1–4

## Opening Encouragement

Families and households often carry great responsibility, pressure, and spiritual weight.

Homes need wisdom, peace, forgiveness, patience, healing, and spiritual strength.

Prayer invites God's peace, guidance, and grace into everyday family life.

## Teaching

Scripture teaches that God cares deeply about households and future generations.

Healthy homes are built intentionally through love, wisdom, prayer, humility, truth, and grace.

Prayer helps strengthen relationships, protect hearts, and bring peace into the home.

## Prayer

Father,

Thank You for families, marriages, children, parents, caregivers, and future generations.

Let Your peace, wisdom, healing, grace, and protection rest upon our households.

Strengthen our homes with unity, compassion, patience, forgiveness, and healthy communication.

Give parents and caregivers wisdom, discernment, humility, and consistency.

Protect children and young people from harmful influences, confusion, fear, and destructive patterns.

Help our homes become places of peace, encouragement, truth, prayer, and spiritual growth.

As for us and our households, we will serve the Lord.

In Jesus' name,

Amen.

## Declarations

- God's peace rests upon my household.
- My home will reflect wisdom, grace, and truth.
- God strengthens families and future generations.
- I walk in forgiveness, humility, and compassion.
- The love of God grows within me daily.
- My relationships are strengthened through wisdom and grace.
- God gives parents wisdom and discernment.

- My household is strengthened through prayer and truth.

## Reflect and Respond

- What areas of your household need greater peace or healing?
- How can you help strengthen communication and unity within your home?
- What habits can help your household grow spiritually?
- What relationships need greater patience, forgiveness, or grace?

## Corporate Prayer

Father,

Strengthen homes and families throughout every generation.

Heal wounded relationships and restore peace where there has been division.

Protect children and young people.

Strengthen parents, caregivers, mentors, and leaders with wisdom and grace.

May our homes become places of peace, truth, encouragement, and spiritual growth.

In Jesus' name,

Amen.

# CHAPTER 10

# PRAYER FOR WALKING IN LOVE AND UNITY

## Foundation Scriptures

- Ephesians 4:31–32
- Colossians 3:12–15
- 1 Corinthians 13
- John 13:34–35
- Romans 12:18

## Opening Encouragement

Relationships require grace, humility, forgiveness, patience, and love.

Without intentional spiritual growth, offense, pride, bitterness, and division can quietly damage relationships and communities.

## Teaching

Scripture teaches believers to walk in love, forgive one another, and endeavor to keep the unity of the Spirit in the bond of peace.

Love is more than emotion. Biblical love involves humility, patience, compassion, wisdom, truth, and maturity.

Prayer helps believers guard their hearts and respond with grace instead of offense.

## Prayer

Father,

Thank You for teaching us to walk in love, forgiveness, humility, and peace.

Help me reflect the character of Jesus Christ in my relationships, conversations, leadership, and responses.

Remove bitterness, pride, offense, jealousy, resentment, and selfish ambition.

Teach me to forgive quickly and walk in compassion.

Help me speak with wisdom, patience, gentleness, and truth.

Strengthen unity throughout homes, churches, friendships, workplaces, and communities.

Let Your love grow within me daily.

Help me become a person who strengthens peace instead of division.

In Jesus' name,

Amen.

## Declarations

- I walk in love, humility, and peace.
- God helps me forgive quickly.
- The love of Christ grows within me daily.
- I reflect wisdom, patience, and compassion.

- The peace of God rules in my heart.
- I speak truth with grace and maturity.
- Unity and peace grow within my relationships.
- The Holy Spirit helps me walk in love.

## Reflect and Respond

- Are there relationships that need forgiveness or healing?
- What attitudes may be affecting peace or unity?
- How can you become more intentional about walking in love?
- What would change if grace governed your responses more consistently?

## Corporate Prayer

Father,

Teach Your people to walk in love, humility, wisdom, forgiveness, and peace.

Remove bitterness, pride, division, offense, and unhealthy conflict.

Strengthen unity throughout homes, churches, workplaces, schools, and communities.

Help believers reflect the wisdom, compassion, and character of Jesus Christ.

In Jesus' name,

Amen.

# CHAPTER 11

# PRAYER FOR THE NEXT GENERATION

## Foundation Scriptures

- Joel 2:28–29
- Acts 2:17
- Proverbs 22:6
- 1 Timothy 4:12
- Psalm 145:4

## Opening Encouragement

The next generation needs wisdom, guidance, encouragement, spiritual strength, and healthy leadership.

Young people face pressure, confusion, distraction, fear, and competing influences daily.

Prayer helps strengthen future generations with purpose, truth, identity, and hope.

## Teaching

Scripture teaches that God desires to pour out His Spirit upon all flesh.

Throughout the Bible, God uses young people for leadership, service, wisdom, courage, and spiritual impact.

Prayer helps create spiritual covering, encouragement, and direction for future generations.

## Prayer

Father,

Thank You for children, students, teenagers, and young adults.

Strengthen this generation with wisdom, courage, spiritual hunger, discernment, identity, and purpose.

Protect young people from confusion, fear, hopelessness, unhealthy influences, addiction, deception, and destructive patterns.

Raise up mentors, teachers, parents, pastors, and leaders who will guide this generation with wisdom, compassion, truth, and integrity.

Let revival spread throughout schools, campuses, homes, churches, and communities.

Strengthen young people to walk with boldness, humility, leadership, and spiritual maturity.

May this generation reflect the wisdom, truth, and love of Jesus Christ.

In Jesus' name,

Amen.

## Declarations

- God is pouring out His Spirit upon this generation.

- Young people are strengthened with wisdom and purpose.
- Sons and daughters will walk in truth and spiritual hunger.
- God is raising up leaders with courage and integrity.
- Revival and spiritual awakening are spreading throughout generations.
- Young people are protected, guided, and strengthened by God.
- The light of the gospel shines into hearts and minds.
- Future generations will reflect truth, wisdom, and compassion.

## Reflect and Respond

- How can you pray more intentionally for young people?
- What influences are shaping the next generation today?
- How can mentors and leaders better support young people?
- What role can you play in strengthening future generations?

## Corporate Prayer

Father,

Pour out Your Spirit upon children, students, teenagers, and young adults.

Strengthen this generation with wisdom, courage, discernment, humility, and purpose.

Raise up healthy leaders, mentors, teachers, pastors, and parents.

Protect future generations from deception, hopelessness, confusion, and destructive influences.

And may this generation reflect the wisdom and love of Jesus Christ throughout the earth.

In Jesus' name,

Amen.

# CHAPTER 12

# PRAYER FOR LEADERS AND DECISION MAKERS

## Foundation Scriptures

- James 1:5
- Proverbs 11:14
- Colossians 1:9
- 1 Timothy 2:1–2
- Proverbs 3:5–6

## Opening Encouragement

Leadership carries responsibility, influence, pressure, and accountability.

Leaders need wisdom, humility, discernment, endurance, peace, and spiritual strength.

Prayer helps leaders remain grounded and spiritually healthy while serving others faithfully.

## Teaching

Throughout Scripture, leaders were encouraged to seek wisdom from God.

Healthy leadership requires humility, teachability, discernment, integrity, patience, and wise counsel.

Prayer strengthens leaders inwardly and helps them lead with wisdom instead of pressure or fear.

## Prayer

Father,

Thank You for every leader, teacher, pastor, parent, mentor, administrator, coach, and decision maker entrusted with responsibility.

Grant wisdom, discernment, humility, courage, peace, and integrity.

Protect leaders from confusion, pride, discouragement, temptation, and emotional exhaustion.

Surround leaders with wise counsel, accountability, encouragement, and spiritual support.

Strengthen leaders to serve faithfully with compassion, wisdom, humility, and truth.

Raise up leaders who reflect the character and wisdom of Jesus Christ.

In Jesus' name,

Amen.

## Declarations

- God gives wisdom to leaders.
- Leaders are strengthened with peace and discernment.
- Humility and integrity guide healthy leadership.
- God surrounds leaders with wise counsel.
- Leaders walk in wisdom instead of fear.
- The Holy Spirit strengthens leaders inwardly.
- God grants endurance and clarity.

- Healthy leadership grows throughout homes and communities.

## Reflect and Respond

- What pressures currently affect leaders in your life?
- How can prayer strengthen leadership more consistently?
- What qualities define healthy leadership?
- How can leaders remain spiritually healthy during pressure?

## Corporate Prayer

Father,

Strengthen leaders throughout homes, churches, schools, organizations, and communities.

Grant wisdom, discernment, peace, humility, and integrity.

Protect leaders from discouragement, pride, confusion, and emotional exhaustion.

Raise up healthy leaders who reflect the wisdom and character of Jesus Christ.

In Jesus' name,

Amen.

## SECTION CLOSING ENCOURAGEMENT

Strong relationships do not happen accidentally.

Homes, families, friendships, churches, and communities grow healthier when prayer, wisdom, humility, forgiveness, grace, and truth remain present.

Continue praying for the people connected to your life.

God is able to strengthen relationships, restore peace, and guide future generations with wisdom and grace.

# SECTION IV

# KINGDOM LIVING AND SPIRITUAL IMPACT

God strengthens believers not only to survive difficult seasons, but to live with courage, wisdom, compassion, and spiritual influence.

These prayers focus on boldness, spiritual awakening, revival, leadership, and the work of the Holy Spirit throughout homes, churches, and communities.

# CHAPTER 13

# PRAYER FOR BOLDNESS AND OPEN DOORS

## Foundation Scriptures

- Acts 4:29–31
- Ephesians 6:18–20
- Colossians 4:2–6
- Psalm 46:1–2
- 2 Timothy 1:7

## Opening Encouragement

There are moments in life when believers need courage to continue moving forward.

Fear, pressure, criticism, uncertainty, and discouragement can cause people to shrink back from opportunities, leadership, service, or purpose.

Yet God strengthens His people with wisdom, courage, and spiritual confidence.

## Teaching

Biblical boldness is not arrogance. It is confidence rooted in truth, humility, and dependence upon God.

The early church prayed for boldness during seasons of pressure and opposition. Instead of becoming consumed by fear, they asked God to strengthen them.

Prayer helps believers remain courageous, spiritually grounded, and faithful during difficult seasons.

## Prayer

Father,

Thank You that You have not given me the spirit of fear, but of power, love, and a sound mind.

Strengthen me with wisdom, courage, humility, and spiritual clarity.

Help me not shrink back because of fear, insecurity, criticism, pressure, or discouragement.

Give me courage to obey You faithfully.

Help me speak truth with wisdom, compassion, humility, and grace.

Open the right doors according to Your purpose.

Lead me into opportunities where I may encourage, strengthen, serve, and reflect the character of Jesus Christ.

Strengthen me inwardly through the Holy Spirit.

Help me remain spiritually steady during seasons of pressure.

Thank You that You are with me wherever I go.

Let my words bring wisdom, encouragement, healing, and grace.

Help me reflect the boldness, wisdom, and love of Jesus Christ.

In Jesus' name,

Amen.

## Declarations

- God has not given me the spirit of fear.
- I walk in courage, wisdom, and humility.
- The Holy Spirit strengthens me inwardly.
- God opens the right doors at the right time.
- I speak truth with grace and wisdom.
- Fear does not control my purpose.
- God strengthens my heart with courage.
- My life reflects the character of Jesus Christ.

## Reflect and Respond

- What fears or insecurities may be affecting your courage?
- Are there opportunities God may be calling you to step into?
- How can you grow in wisdom and boldness together?
- What pressures currently tempt you to shrink back?

## Corporate Prayer

Father,

Strengthen Your people with courage, wisdom, peace, and discernment.

Remove fear, insecurity, confusion, discouragement, and unhealthy striving.

Open doors for encouragement, leadership, service, healing, and truth.

Help believers reflect the character and wisdom of Jesus Christ throughout every sphere of influence.

In Jesus' name,

Amen.

# CHAPTER 14

# PRAYER FOR THE OUTPOURING OF THE HOLY SPIRIT

## Foundation Scriptures

- Joel 2:28–29
- Acts 2:17–18
- 2 Chronicles 7:14
- Habakkuk 3:2
- Isaiah 44:3

## Opening Encouragement

Throughout Scripture, God repeatedly moved among people who were humble, prayerful, hungry, and surrendered.

Revival produces repentance, spiritual hunger, humility, transformation, compassion, and renewed passion for God.

Prayer for revival begins with hearts that remain open and responsive before God.

## Teaching

God still desires to move within homes, churches, schools, campuses, communities, and nations.

Revival is not produced merely through programs or personalities. Spiritual awakening grows where there is humility, surrender, prayer, repentance, and dependence upon God.

Prayer helps believers remain spiritually hungry, teachable, and sensitive to the Holy Spirit.

## Prayer

Father,

Thank You that You are still moving by Your Spirit today.

Pour out Your Spirit upon homes, churches, schools, campuses, communities, and nations.

Awaken hearts toward truth, repentance, wisdom, humility, prayer, and spiritual hunger.

Revive Your people again.

Renew our love for Your presence and Your Word.

Remove spiritual apathy, pride, compromise, distraction, bitterness, and division.

Pour out Your Spirit upon children, teenagers, young adults, families, leaders, and future generations.

Raise up people who hunger for truth, prayer, wisdom, compassion, and spiritual maturity.

Bring healing where there is brokenness.

Bring peace where there is confusion.

Bring hope where there is discouragement.

Help believers reflect the character of Jesus Christ everywhere they go.

And let revival produce lasting transformation throughout homes, churches, and communities.

In Jesus' name,

Amen.

## Declarations

- God is pouring out His Spirit upon all flesh.
- Revival and spiritual awakening are spreading throughout generations.
- The Holy Spirit renews hearts and minds.
- Spiritual hunger is increasing throughout homes and communities.
- Young people are being strengthened with wisdom and purpose.
- The light of the gospel shines throughout this generation.
- God is renewing His people with grace and truth.
- The Church will reflect the character and love of Jesus Christ.

## Reflect and Respond

- What areas of your life need spiritual renewal?
- How can you become more intentional about prayer and spiritual hunger?
- What distractions may be affecting your sensitivity to the Holy Spirit?
- How can you pray more consistently for revival within your community?

## Corporate Prayer

Father,

Pour out Your Spirit upon homes, churches, schools, campuses, communities, and nations.

Awaken spiritual hunger throughout every generation.

Strengthen believers with humility, wisdom, truth, compassion, courage, and discernment.

Heal brokenness, restore hope, renew minds, and strengthen relationships.

Raise up leaders, mentors, pastors, teachers, parents, and servants who reflect the wisdom and character of Jesus Christ.

And may the light of the gospel shine brightly throughout this generation and those to come.

In Jesus' name,

Amen.

## SECTION CLOSING ENCOURAGEMENT

God desires His people to live with courage, compassion, wisdom, humility, and spiritual impact.

Continue praying for revival, renewal, and spiritual awakening throughout homes, churches, schools, communities, and future generations.

God is still able to pour out His Spirit upon all flesh.

# APPENDIX A

# THE EPISTLE PRAYERS IN PRAYER FORM

The prayers found throughout the New Testament epistles provide believers with powerful examples of how to pray according to the wisdom, purposes, and will of God.

These prayers emphasize:

- wisdom
- revelation
- spiritual growth
- love
- strength
- endurance
- discernment
- peace
- unity
- maturity
- These prayer forms are designed for personal devotion, family prayer, mentoring, prayer groups, leadership settings, and spiritual growth.
- EPHESIANS 1:17–19
- Prayer for Wisdom and Revelation
- Father,
- Grant unto us the spirit of wisdom and revelation in the knowledge of You.

- Open the eyes of our understanding.
- Help us know the hope of Your calling and the greatness of Your power toward those who believe.
- Strengthen us to walk in wisdom, discernment, humility, and spiritual maturity.
- In Jesus' name,
- Amen.
- EPHESIANS 3:14–21
- Prayer for Spiritual Strength and Rooted Love
- Father,
- Strengthen us with might through Your Spirit in the inner man.
- Root and ground us in love.
- Help us comprehend the depth and greatness of the love of Christ.
- Fill us with wisdom, peace, grace, and spiritual strength.
- Thank You that You are able to do exceedingly abundantly above all we ask or think.
- In Jesus' name,
- Amen.
- PHILIPPIANS 1:9–11
- Prayer for Love and Discernment
- Father,
- Let our love abound more and more in knowledge and discernment.
- Help us approve the things that are excellent and walk sincerely before You.
- Teach us to walk in wisdom, humility, compassion, and spiritual maturity.

- In Jesus' name,
- Amen.
- COLOSSIANS 1:9–12
- Prayer for Wisdom and Fruitfulness
- Father,
- Fill us with the knowledge of Your will in all wisdom and spiritual understanding.
- Help us walk worthy of the Lord and be fruitful in every good work.
- Strengthen us with endurance, patience, wisdom, and joy.
- In Jesus' name,
- Amen.
- 2 THESSALONIANS 1:11–12
- Prayer for Calling and Spiritual Strength
- Father,
- Strengthen us to accomplish the good things You have called us to do.
- Help us live lives worthy of Your calling.
- May our lives honor Jesus Christ in every area.
- In Jesus' name,
- Amen.
- HEBREWS 13:20–21
- Prayer for Spiritual Maturity and Obedience
- Father,
- Equip us with everything good for doing Your will.
- Work within us and shape our lives according to Your wisdom and purpose.
- Help us reflect the character of Jesus Christ in our daily lives.

- In Jesus' name,
- Amen.

# APPENDIX B

# SCRIPTURAL BLESSINGS AND DECLARATIONS

These declarations are designed to help believers pray, meditate upon, and agree with the promises and truth of Scripture.

## Peace and Trust

The peace of God guards my heart and mind.

God has not given me the spirit of fear.

I walk in peace, wisdom, and spiritual stability.

God is my refuge and strength.

I trust the Lord one day at a time.

The Holy Spirit strengthens me inwardly.

## Wisdom and Direction

God gives wisdom generously.

The Holy Spirit leads and guides me.

I walk in wisdom, discernment, and clarity.

God directs my paths faithfully.

My mind is renewed through the Word of God.

Wisdom grows within me daily.

## Healing and Restoration

God is my Healer and Restorer.

God renews my strength daily.

I walk in peace, healing, and restoration.

God restores what has been wounded or broken.

The grace of God sustains me.

God is faithful throughout every season.

## Families and Relationships

As for me and my house, we will serve the Lord.

God's peace rests upon my household.

My home will reflect love, wisdom, and truth.

I walk in forgiveness, humility, and compassion.

The love of God grows within me daily.

My relationships are strengthened through wisdom and grace.

## Boldness and Spiritual Impact

God has not given me the spirit of fear.

I walk in courage, wisdom, and humility.

God opens the right doors at the right time.

I speak truth with grace and wisdom.

Fear does not control my purpose.

My life reflects the character of Jesus Christ.

## Revival and Spiritual Hunger

God is pouring out His Spirit upon all flesh.

Revival and spiritual awakening are spreading throughout generations.

Spiritual hunger is increasing throughout homes and communities.

The Holy Spirit renews hearts and minds.

God is faithful to awaken hearts again.

The Church will reflect the character and love of Jesus Christ.

## Priestly Blessing

## Numbers 6:24–26

The Lord bless you and keep you.

The Lord make His face shine upon you and be gracious to you.

The Lord lift up His countenance upon you and give you peace.

Amen.

# APPENDIX C

# CORPORATE PRAYER MODELS

These corporate prayer models are designed to help groups pray together with unity, wisdom, humility, and spiritual focus.

## Corporate Prayer for Wisdom and Direction

Father,

Give Your people wisdom, clarity, peace, and discernment.

Guide leaders, families, students, churches, and communities according to Your wisdom.

Remove confusion, fear, distraction, and instability.

Teach us to trust You and acknowledge You in all our ways.

In Jesus' name,

Amen.

## Corporate Prayer for Families and Households

Father,

Strengthen homes, marriages, children, parents, caregivers, and future generations.

Bring peace, healing, wisdom, protection, and unity throughout our households.

Help our homes become places of prayer, encouragement, truth, and spiritual growth.

In Jesus' name,

Amen.

## Corporate Prayer for the Next Generation

Father,

Strengthen children, students, teenagers, and young adults with wisdom, courage, purpose, and spiritual hunger.

Protect future generations from deception, hopelessness, confusion, and destructive influences.

Raise up mentors, leaders, teachers, pastors, and parents who will guide this generation with wisdom and compassion.

In Jesus' name,

Amen.

## Corporate Prayer for Healing and Restoration

Father,

Bring healing throughout homes, families, churches, and communities.

Strengthen those who are grieving, discouraged, wounded, anxious, or emotionally exhausted.

Restore peace, unity, hope, wisdom, and spiritual strength.

In Jesus' name,

Amen.

## Corporate Prayer for Leaders

Father,

Strengthen leaders with wisdom, humility, discernment, peace, and integrity.

Protect leaders from discouragement, confusion, pride, and emotional exhaustion.

Raise up healthy leaders who reflect the wisdom and character of Jesus Christ.

In Jesus' name,

Amen.

## Corporate Prayer for Revival

Father,

Pour out Your Spirit upon homes, churches, schools, campuses, and communities.

Awaken spiritual hunger throughout every generation.

Strengthen believers with wisdom, humility, truth, compassion, and courage.

May revival spread with love, healing, truth, and transformation.

In Jesus' name,

Amen.

# APPENDIX D

# DAILY PRAYER RHYTHM GUIDE

Prayer is meant to become part of the rhythm of everyday life.

Healthy prayer rhythms help believers remain spiritually grounded, renew the mind, strengthen faith, grow in peace, and walk intentionally.

## Morning Prayer Rhythm

Morning prayer helps believers begin the day with:

- gratitude
- surrender
- wisdom
- peace
- spiritual focus

## Suggested morning focus:

- thank God for His faithfulness
- surrender the day to God
- ask for wisdom and peace
- renew the mind through Scripture
- pray for others

## Midday Prayer Rhythm

Midday prayer helps believers:

- refocus spiritually
- release stress

- renew peace
- remain aware of God throughout the day

## Suggested midday prayer:

"Father, renew my mind and strengthen me inwardly through the Holy Spirit. Help me walk in peace, wisdom, patience, and discernment throughout this day."

## Evening Prayer Rhythm

Evening prayer helps believers:

- release burdens
- reflect honestly
- forgive quickly
- give thanks
- rest peacefully

## Suggested evening focus:

- thank God for the day
- release burdens and anxiety
- practice forgiveness
- pray for protection and peace
- rest in God's faithfulness

## Weekly Reflection Questions

- What has God been teaching me recently?
- What areas need greater surrender?
- What distractions need to be removed?
- Where have I seen God's faithfulness?
- How can I grow spiritually in the coming week?

## Final Encouragement

Prayer is not about performance.

Prayer is relationship.

Continue showing up faithfully before God.

Continue returning to the Word.

Continue growing one prayer at a time.

# FINAL BLESSING

May the Word of God form your prayers.

May the grace of God steady your heart.

May the peace of God guard your mind.

May the wisdom of God direct your steps.

May the love of Christ shape your relationships.

May the Holy Spirit strengthen you inwardly, guide you faithfully, and help you walk in truth.

May your home be filled with peace.

May your life be marked by purpose.

May your prayers be rooted in Scripture, shaped by grace, and lifted in faith.

May prayer become more than something you practice occasionally.

May prayer become a lifestyle formed by the Word of God.

The Lord bless you and keep you.

The Lord make His face shine upon you and be gracious to you.

The Lord lift up His countenance upon you and give you peace.

In Jesus' name,

Amen.

# ACKNOWLEDGMENTS

With gratitude to every mentor, teacher, pastor, leader, parent, intercessor, and believer who continues helping others grow in faith, wisdom, prayer, and spiritual maturity.

Thank you to those who continue strengthening homes, churches, schools, communities, and future generations through consistent prayer, encouragement, service, leadership, and love.

Most importantly, thank You to the Lord Jesus Christ for grace, mercy, wisdom, peace, direction, healing, and the continual work of transformation through the Holy Spirit and the Word of God.

# SCRIPTURE ACKNOWLEDGMENTS

# ABOUT THE AUTHOR

Steven Robertson Sr. is a purpose-driven mentor, educator, speaker, and leader committed to helping people discover purpose, walk intentionally, and grow spiritually through faith, wisdom, leadership, and transformational mentoring.

With decades of experience in education, youth development, college access, ministry, and leadership development, Steven has dedicated his life to helping individuals recognize their God-given potential and take intentional steps toward purpose.

Through Steps On Purpose, his writing, teaching, and mentoring work emphasize faith, formation, leadership, resilience, and living with purpose in every step.

His heart is to encourage believers to walk with clarity, pray with confidence, lead with humility, and become people whose lives reflect the wisdom, love, and grace of Jesus Christ.

www.ingramcontent.com/pod-product-compliance
Lightning Source LLC
LaVergne TN
LVHW041134150826
845673LV00007B/2324

* 9 7 8 1 9 7 2 1 6 5 0 0 3 *